GREEN STREET TEAM

by Mindy Menschell • illustrations by Jeff Shelly

Harcourt Brace & Company

Orlando Atlanta Austin Boston San Francisco Chicago Dallas New York Toronto London

Our team is the Green Street Team. It's a neat team! We meet each week.

Fred helps us. Fred has a lot to teach the team.

Jean is at the net. She can't let another team sneak the ball into our net.

Jean can hit the ball with her feet, knees, heels, chest—any way she can! Jean can use her hands, too. The rest of the team can't.

Today we meet the Kent Street Team. The Kent Street Team isn't weak. We need to play well.

Fred tells us, "You need speed. Run fast. Kick far. Don't let the ball get between your feet!"

Fred helps us check things.
We have clean vests. Jean has
a neat vest with green checks.
Jean's vest isn't a mess—yet!

We each have shoes with cleats for speed. We have shin pads to keep our legs safe. We test the ball to see if it has enough air.

When we are set, we kneel around Fred. No one speaks or makes a peep when Fred gives his pep-talk speech.

"Our Green Street Team is a neat team!" says Fred. "We can be the best team! Yes, we can!"

We greet the Kent Street Team
with a yell:
    Green Street, Kent Street—
    Each team is neat!
    But Green Street, Green
        Street—
    We're the team to beat!

Then the game starts! Kent Street has speed! They get the ball close to our net. But Jean won't let them kick it in. Then our team steals the ball!

Can Kent Street sneak the ball away from Green Street? No way! Green Street kicks the ball into the Kent Street net!

Each team plays its best. But in the end, Green Street beats Kent Street—1 to 0! We shake hands with the Kent Street Team. Then we yell.

Green Street, Green Street!
The best today!
Green Street, the Dream
    Team!
All the way!